FOOD and FARMING

FARMING *and the* ENVIRONMENT

Richard and Louise Spilsbury

PowerKiDS
press™

New York

Published in 2011 by The Rosen Publishing Group Inc.
29 East 21st Street, New York, NY 10010

First Edition

Editor: Julia Adams
Managing Editor, Discovery Books: Rachel Tisdale
Editor, Discovery Books: Jenny Vaughan
Designer and Illustrator: Graham Rich
Picture Researcher: Bobby Humphrey
Consultant: Nicholas Rowles

Library of Congress Cataloging-in-Publication Data

Spilsbury, Richard, 1963-
    Farming and the environment / by Richard and Louise Spilsbury. — 1st ed.
       p. cm. — (Food and farming)
    Includes index.
    ISBN 978-1-61532-577-1 (library binding)
    ISBN 978-1-61532-583-2 (paperback)
    ISBN 978-1-61532-584-9 (6-pack)
    1. Agriculture—Environmental aspects—Juvenile literature. I. Spilsbury, Louise.
    II. Title. III. Series: Food and farming.
    S519.S69 2011
    630.28'6—dc22

                            2009045750

Manufactured in China

Photographs:
Alamy Images: p. 16 Julia Waterlow/Eye Ubiquitous; Florida Fish and Wildlife Commission:
p. 24 (Tim Donovan); Getty Images: pp. 6 (Joseph J. Scherschel/National Geographic),
8 (Sylvain Grandadam/The Image Bank), 10 (Tom Stoddart Archive), 14 (Hoang Dinh
Nam/AFP), 17 (Peter Essick/Aurora), 20 (David McNew), 22 (Torsten Blackwood/AFP),
26 (Travel Ink); Istockphoto.com: pp. 5 (Malcolm Crooks), 7, 12 (Greg Gardner),
23 (Alexander Sporr), 25, 27 (Eric Delmar), 28 (Cathleen Abers-Kimbell); Shutterstock:
pp. 9 (Sasha Radosavljevich), 13 (Alex Franklin), 29, cover top (Hougaard Malan);
Still Pictures: p. 18 & cover top (Ron Giling)

Manufactured in China
CPSIA Compliance Information: Batch #WAS0102PK: For Further Information
contact Rosen Publishing, New York, New York at 1-800-237-9932

CONTENTS

The Farm Ecosystem 4

Farming Interdependency 6

Demand for Water 8

Overuse of Water 10

Spoiling the Water 12

The Effects of Water Pollution 14

Losing Soil 16

The Effects of Soil Erosion 18

Farming and the Atmosphere 20

The Impacts of Air Pollution 22

Land Clearance 24

Ecosystem Impacts 26

Sustainable Farming 28

Glossary 30

Topic Web, Find Out More,
    and Web Sites 31

Index 32

THE FARM ECOSYSTEM

A farm is an ecosystem. This means it is a system of living things and their environment, the relationship between these, and how they affect each other.

Natural Inputs

A farm ecosystem includes crops, livestock (farm animals), and also the wild animals and plants living on a farm, such as insects and weeds. Most farm ecosystems rely on natural inputs. An input is anything that is put into producing things. For example, crops make their food from carbon dioxide gas in the air and water from the soil by a process called photosynthesis, which uses energy from sunlight. To grow well, remain healthy, and produce seeds to create new plants,

crops need to take up minerals and nutrients, many of which are found naturally in the soil. These vital substances include the elements nitrogen, potassium, phosphorus, calcium, and iron. Soil rich in nutrients and minerals is called fertile soil, and it supports the growth of large amounts of crops. Livestock also rely on the soil, since they often eat plants growing on a farm. When crops are harvested and livestock killed, the nutrients that have been removed from the soil are never naturally replaced.

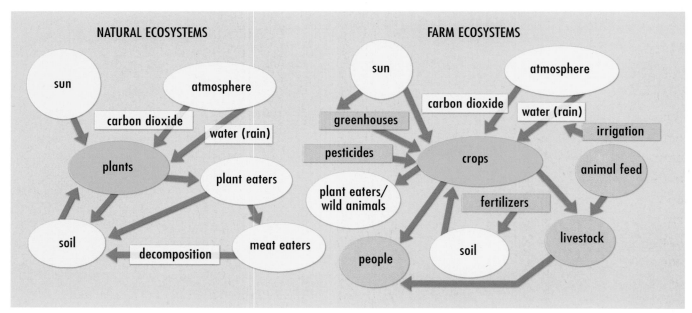

▲ *This diagram shows the differences between a natural ecosystem and a farm ecosystem. The arrows show the inputs and outputs.*

▲ *A farm environment depends on natural inputs, such as rain and the minerals that are found naturally in the soil. The farmer's labor is also an input.*

Human Control

A farm ecosystem is different from, for example, a forest ecosystem, because humans control many of the interactions on the farm. On some farms, the natural inputs may be insufficient to grow enough crops, so farmers add extra water or nutrients to make the soil more fertile. In regions without enough warmth from the sun, farmers may grow crops in heated greenhouses. Naturally occurring living things compete for space and other resources with crops and livestock. For instance, weeds take up space and use nutrients from the soil, and insect pests may eat crops, harm livestock, and cause damage to food. Farmers control the ecosystem by killing or deterring pests.

WORLD FARMLAND

Around 25 percent of the world's land area is used for livestock pasture and 11 percent is used for crops. The amount of land taken up by farms grew by nine percent between 1963 and 1985, but modern farming methods have made it possible for food production to rise by 60 percent.

Interdependency is the word we use for the way living things rely on each other in order to survive. For instance, crops attract insects, such as bees, that collect pollen. They need this for food. The plants benefit, because the bees pollinate flowers.

CASE STUDY

Fish Farming

Farming fish, such as salmon, makes an impact on ocean fish, too. Most farmed fish are fed on feed that is rich in protein. Fish feed is mostly made from ocean fish, including anchovy, herring, whiting, and sand eel. It takes three tons of wild fish to make enough feed to grow just one ton of farmed salmon. The numbers of many wild fish are dropping because of the demand for fish feed. There are fewer fish, not only for people to eat, but also for ocean animals, such as seals.

Farmers and the Ecosystem

Farmers are interdependent with other parts of the farm's ecosystem. For example, when farmers kill pests to protect their crops from damage, they may also kill bees, who fertilize crops. Without bees, the crops may not develop properly, and the farmers' profits suffer. When farmers add nutrients to create fertile soil, rain may wash some of them into rivers, causing pollution. Water pollution can damage the farm and the wildlife on it, as well as communities of people living by rivers, including the farmers themselves. It also affects the ecosystems in the oceans that rivers flow into.

▲ *Cattle are most productive when they have high-quality food to eat. But there is a limit to the amount of grain that can be grown, and the more that is fed to cattle, the less there is for people.*

Consumer Pressure

Farmers depend on consumers, and consumers depend on farmers. Pressures on the environment caused by farming are increased by consumer demand. For instance, in China, people are eating more meat each year as they are getting richer and can afford more. The Chinese are rearing more livestock and importing meat from other countries to meet this demand. Most livestock farmers feed their animals grain. When grain farmers grow more grain for livestock rather than for people, food made from the grain gets more expensive and so poor people may go hungry.

▶ *In the United States, around $15 billion worth of crops are pollinated by bees each year. Without bees, the crops would not be productive. Without crops, the bees could not live.*

DEMAND FOR WATER

Globally, 70 percent of all the fresh water people use goes into agriculture. This is mainly because farmers use so much water when they irrigate (water) fields.

Collecting and Using Water

Irrigation is especially important in parts of the world where the climate is always dry, as well as in other parts of the world where it is dry for part of the year. Under these conditions, farmers cannot rely on rain to supply the water they need. Some farms have their own reservoirs or water tanks that store rainwater. Many others pump water from nearby lakes and rivers, or from underground sources. One-third of all irrigation water is groundwater (water lying deep under the ground) formed after surface water (in lakes and rivers) has trickled through the soil and collected in underground rocks, called aquifers. One-sixth of the world's cropland is irrigated, but it produces one third of the world's food. Livestock also need large volumes of water to drink, and water is used when farmers and food factories process meat and dairy products.

▲ *This worker in Egypt is irrigating a field in a traditional way, allowing river water to flow along ditches, through fields of crops.*

Water-Hungry Crops

Some crops use more water than others. Some of the most water-hungry crops are wheat, corn, and alfalfa. It takes 162,000 gallons (613,000 L) of water to grow just over a ton (1 t) of alfalfa. In California, nearly two-thirds of all alfalfa is grown as dairy cattle feed. This uses about a quarter of all irrigation water in the state. The government of California lets the farmers have water at low prices, in order to encourage agriculture in the state.

Wasting Water

Scientists estimate that around 60 percent of all irrigation water is lost before it reaches any crops. Some is wasted when pipes or sprinklers leak, but most evaporates after it has been sprayed on the soil, especially in hot, dry areas. Evaporation is when energy from the sun's heat or the wind changes liquid water to a gas called water vapor. Farmers who irrigate in the hot daytime use, and lose, large amounts of water. Irrigating at cooler times of the day can save water.

▶ *Like humans, livestock need a good supply of water in order to survive. Dairy cows like these can each drink around 30 gallons (115 L) of water a day.*

OVERUSE OF WATER

The farming industry drains valuable fresh water resources. Without it, farms cannot produce food. However, overuse of water is creating shortages in some areas and spoiling farmland in others.

Drying Up

When rivers, lakes, reservoirs, and aquifers dry up, there is less fresh water for people to use. In poor countries, this can mean that people must travel long distances for water. When they find it, it may be polluted. This puts them at risk of catching waterborne diseases, such as cholera. Overusing water also affects industries such as fishing and river transportation. Surface water supplies, such as lakes and rivers, may quickly recover after rainfall, but groundwater takes longer. As aquifers empty, wells dry up and soil dries out. In Tianjin, in northern China, so much groundwater has been removed that it has affected the soil, and buildings are sinking into the ground.

◄ *These people in Tanzania, East Africa, are collecting water from a communal faucet. Water supplies in poor countries are often less plentiful than in rich ones, and overuse by agriculture can result in a lack of drinking water.*

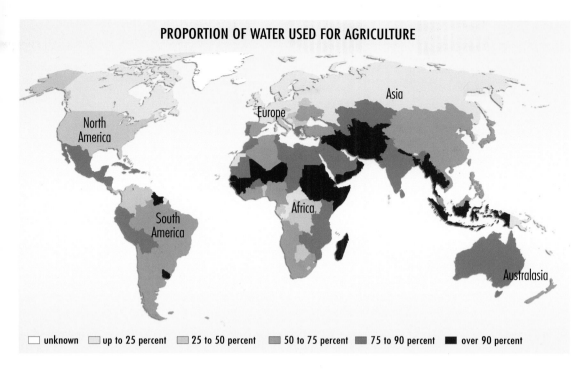

PROPORTION OF WATER USED FOR AGRICULTURE

North America
Europe
Asia
South America
Africa
Australasia

☐ unknown ☐ up to 25 percent ☐ 25 to 50 percent ☐ 50 to 75 percent ☐ 75 to 90 percent ■ over 90 percent

◀ *This map shows which parts of the world use the largest proportion of their water for agriculture. Using large amounts of water for irrigation can lead to supply problems for use in people's homes.*

Salty Fields

Rainwater and groundwater contain small amounts of dissolved salts. When fields cannot drain properly, plants take up water but leave the salts behind. Salts build up in the soil and make it hard for new plants to take up the water and nutrients they need. When people drill deep into the rocks to find groundwater, they bring dissolved salts from underground rocks to the surface. These wash into surface water supplies, making water for livestock and irrigation saltier. This is called salination and it can make water too salty for crops to grow or for livestock to drink.

CASE STUDY

Disappearing Lake

Lake Chad, in Central Africa, has shrunk to one-twentieth of its size since 1963. The most dramatic fall in size has happened since 1983, when irrigation schemes were set up to supply water to grow rice in the region. So much was taken from the lake that there was no longer enough left for local subsistence farmers (farmers who grow food mainly for their own families) to use. It also affected livestock herders, who no longer had enough water for their animals, and fishermen who had been using the lake to catch fish.

SPOILING THE WATER

When crops are grown on the same land year after year, they use up the nutrients that occur naturally in the soil. Farmers use inputs of different kinds to keep the soil productive. However, these can harm the environment.

Sources of Pollution

The inputs that farmers use are manure and large amounts of agrochemicals (chemicals used in agriculture). These are usually fertilizers produced in chemical factories, and are mixtures of nitrates (which supply nitrogen to plants), phosphates (which supply phosphorus), and potash (which supplies potassium). Farmers often prefer agrochemicals to manure because they can apply the correct quantities in order to grow the best crops. Other kinds of agrochemicals are herbicides (weed killers) and pesticides, which destroy organisms that damage crops or livestock. Overuse of these chemicals damages water sources.

▲ *On large farms, liquid pesticides or fertilizers can be sprayed on the land using aircraft. On smaller farms, the chemicals are applied with tractors or by hand.*

Heavy rain may wash soil into rivers, and with it, chemical fertilizers and manure. This pollutes the water and leaves the soil poorer.

From Field to Water

Where there is high annual rainfall, or where there are often bursts of heavy rain, there can be a serious problem of agricultural runoff. This is when rainwater washes manure and chemicals into rivers and other water sources. It is made worse if, for example, the fields slope steeply. The type of soil is also important. Sandy soil allows water to soak through it twice as quickly as clay. This means that agrochemicals, too, will soak deep into sandy soil and do not readily enter surface water sources.

THE MANURE PROBLEM

On intensive livestock farms, many animals live together in small spaces. They create a lot of manure, which is stored in pits or lakes as slurry. Livestock in the United States produce 130 times more waste than all the people living there. In many parts of the world, there are strict regulations to make sure farmers prevent this waste getting into rivers. A safe way to dispose of slurry is to spread it thinly over large areas of farmland, where it gradually soaks into the soil and breaks down before entering the water system. However, this is expensive, which means that some farmers dump slurry illegally. This may pollute water resources.

Water pollution has many consequences in and beyond the farm ecosystem. It can transform river ecosystems and make freshwater resources unavailable or dangerous for people or wildlife. This can happen in a number of ways.

Bloom

Bloom is the rapid growth and reproduction of algae in water. Algae are tiny organisms. Like crops, they grow faster in the presence of nitrates and phosphates. When the algae die, billions of bacteria feed on them and, as these respire (breathe), they use up much of the oxygen dissolved in water. Then there is not enough oxygen for aquatic animals such as fish and frogs to survive. This is called eutrophication.

EUTROPHICATION

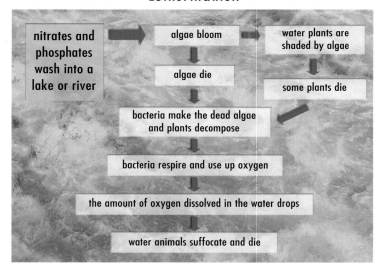

nitrates and phosphates wash into a lake or river

algae bloom

water plants are shaded by algae

algae die

some plants die

bacteria make the dead algae and plants decompose

bacteria respire and use up oxygen

the amount of oxygen dissolved in the water drops

water animals suffocate and die

▲ *This diagram shows how eutrophication happens when agrochemicals get into rivers and lakes.*

CASE STUDY

River Death

In November 1991, the largest river toxic algal bloom in history occurred in the Barwon and Darling rivers in New South Wales, Australia. From the air, the bloom looked like a wide green ribbon, estimated to be around 620 miles (1,000 km) long. This was the result of very low water levels, flowing very slowly because so much had been taken for irrigation. The government declared a state of emergency, partly because livestock had died after drinking the water.

Dangerous Water

Water pollution caused by farming can have several dangerous effects on human health. Blooms of certain types of algae can produce chemicals that make the skin blister, or cause vomiting, diarrhea, sore eyes, and breathing problems when people wash in, or drink, polluted water. Fertilizers and substances in slurry, such as bacteria and livestock medicines, may also accumulate in freshwater supplies and make the water dangerous to drink. High nitrate levels can cause blue baby syndrome, when infants cannot breathe properly and may even die. Treating polluted water to make it safe for people to use is expensive and is therefore not always possible in poor countries.

▼ *Farmers in poor countries, such as this rice grower in Thailand, may overuse many agrochemicals in an attempt to increase yields. As a result, they can end up damaging the environment.*

15

LOSING SOIL

Good soil is necessary if farmers are to grow healthy crops or raise livestock. Yet it can be lost when water or winds carry it away. This is called soil erosion, and it is a major global problem, made worse by the way some farmers treat their land.

Surface Soil

Soil erosion affects the surface layer of soil, or topsoil. Topsoil contains humus, which is a spongy material that forms when bacteria and other soil organisms break down the remains of living things. Humus binds together rock particles in soil and absorbs water. Animals, such as earthworms, mix the humus with the topsoil as they move through it. Fertile, humus-rich soil releases nutrients that plant roots can take up. Topsoil develops slowly. It takes about 300 years to reach a depth of 1 inch (2.5 cm).

SOIL EROSION WORLDWIDE

More than 25 million acres (10 million ha) of productive soil are lost worldwide each year and an area ten times the size of Michigan becomes too barren to produce food. Globally, topsoil is eroding faster than it can be replaced in over a third of the world's croplands. In the United States, topsoil loss costs around $125 billion every year.

▲ *Erosion can easily happen on steep hillsides, but it can be prevented by making terraces and planting trees on them, as it has been done here, in China. The trees' roots will then hold the soil firmly in place.*

▲ *When there is too much livestock on the same piece of land, they trample the soil, destroying its structure and also the plants, whose roots hold the soil together. Erosion can quickly follow as wind and rain carry the exposed soil away.*

Wasting Soil Resources

Soil erosion can happen when land is cleared of natural vegetation, such as hedges and trees, including forests. Wind, rain, and floods carry the topsoil away. Soil erosion can also happen as a result of poor farming practices. For example, if a farmer plows sloping land from top to bottom rather than side to side, this creates pathways for the soil to wash downward. It is made worse if the farmer grows too many crops, which exhaust the nutrients in the topsoil. The humus breaks down and the soil easily crumbles and erodes.

THE EFFECTS OF SOIL EROSION

When soil is eroded, the land left behind is not fertile. Crops cannot grow well, and the eroded soil builds up away from its original position, often creating more problems.

Making Deserts

When eroded land with little topsoil becomes infertile, and not moist enough for plants to grow, we call this desertification. Desertification happens when plants disappear after livestock overgraze land, or people collect plants to feed livestock or to burn for cooking and heating. With no plant roots or humus, soil turns to dust. Over the past 50 years, an area of around 247,000 square miles (640,000 sq km) has become desert at the southern edge of the Sahara. This is about the same size as the entire country of Somalia. In many parts of the world, dust causes health problems for people, such as eye and lung infections.

▲ *This woman in Thailand is cultivating soil that has already been cleared. Trees have been cut down or burned, putting the whole area at risk of soil erosion.*

Soil in Water

Land may flood if eroded topsoil chokes the channels and rivers that rainfall usually drains into. Soil may choke pipes in hydroelectric power stations, or damage their turbines, so that they cannot produce as much electricity as they should. Soil can also damage natural ecosystems, such as coral reefs. These are underwater structures that are home to a vast range of marine organisms. The soil smothers the reef and kills the tiny animals from which the coral is formed. The whole ecosystem can be destroyed.

THE WORST AREAS FOR EROSION

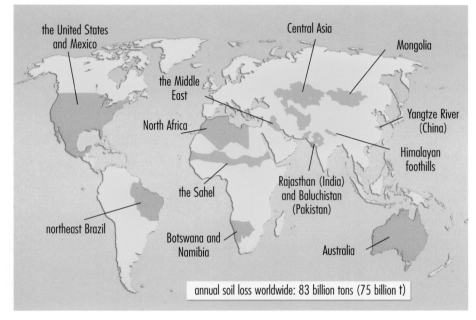

the United States and Mexico

Central Asia

Mongolia

the Middle East

North Africa

Yangtze River (China)

the Sahel

Rajasthan (India) and Baluchistan (Pakistan)

Himalayan foothills

northeast Brazil

Botswana and Namibia

Australia

annual soil loss worldwide: 83 billion tons (75 billion t)

CAUSES OF EROSION

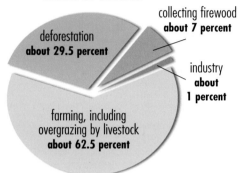

deforestation **about 29.5 percent**

collecting firewood **about 7 percent**

industry **about 1 percent**

farming, including overgrazing by livestock **about 62.5 percent**

▲ *Farming, including grazing livestock, is responsible for around two-thirds of soil erosion.*

◄ *This map shows the parts of the world where the most soil erosion is taking place.*

CASE STUDY

Dust Bowl

In the 1920s, many settlers created farms on prairie grassland in the United States. Their steel plows broke up the tough grass roots. Then, in the 1930s, there were several years of drought. With nothing to hold the soil in place, an area of Kansas, Texas, Oklahoma, and other states measuring 154,440 square miles (400,000 square km) lost its topsoil. It was called the Dust Bowl, because clouds of dusty soil filled the sky. Hundreds of thousands of farming families had to leave their land and move to other parts of the United States.

FARMING AND THE ATMOSPHERE

The farming industry produces large quantities of gases that enter the atmosphere. The two most significant sources of these gases are the various kinds of farm machinery and livestock farming.

Vehicles and Machinery

Greenhouse gases are gases that store heat from the sun, and keep our planet warm. One of the most important of these gases is carbon dioxide. Some of this comes from burning fuel. Fuel is burned by farm machinery, such as tractors and the vehicles used to collect and deliver food. Farm machines may also use electricity, which is often created by power stations that burn fuels such as coal or gas. These also produce carbon dioxide.

Livestock

Other greenhouse gases include methane, nitrous oxide, and ammonia. Globally, livestock production releases over a third of all methane emissions that are related to human activities. These are 23 times as warming as carbon dioxide. Livestock also accounts for around two-thirds of human-related emissions of both nitrous oxide and of ammonia. These are produced by the activity of bacteria in manure, and they store more heat for longer than carbon dioxide. For instance, nitrous oxide is nearly 300 times better at storing heat than carbon dioxide.

FOOTPRINTS

The carbon footprint of farmed food is the total amount of carbon dioxide and other greenhouse gases emitted during its production. For example, the carbon footprint of salad grown in a greenhouse may include emissions from fuel used to heat the greenhouse and used by vehicles that transport the salad to stores. Farmers growing crops also take into account the carbon dioxide plants take in from the atmosphere when they make their food by photosynthesis. A study of a Scottish farm calculated that the 128 tons (116 t) of barley grown on the farm removed 47.7 tons (43.3 t) of carbon from the atmosphere.

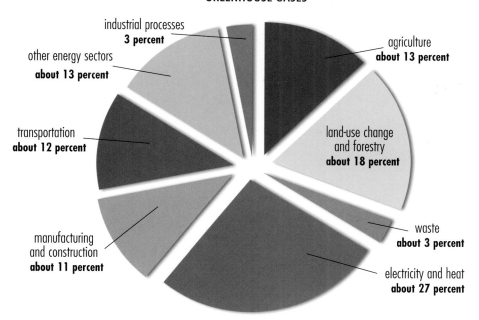

GREENHOUSE GASES

industrial processes
3 percent

other energy sectors
about 13 percent

transportation
about 12 percent

manufacturing
and construction
about 11 percent

agriculture
about 13 percent

land-use change
and forestry
about 18 percent

waste
about 3 percent

electricity and heat
about 27 percent

◄ *This chart shows the proportions of greenhouse gases produced by different human activities. We can see that farming creates around the same proportion as transportation.*

▼ *When farm machines burn fuels made from oil, they emit exhaust fumes. These contain gases such as carbon dioxide, adding to the amount of greenhouse gases agriculture creates.*

THE IMPACTS OF AIR POLLUTION

Weather patterns around the world are changing. Nearly all scientists agree that this is because the level of greenhouse gases in the atmosphere is increasing and trapping more heat.

Climate Change

Green plants remove carbon dioxide from the atmosphere. However, human activity, such as burning oil, is increasing the level of carbon dioxide faster than the plants can remove it. Scientists believe that this increase in a major greenhouse gas is causing global warming (a rise in the average global temperatures), which is affecting general climate patterns. For example, droughts and floods are getting more severe, and an increasing number of the hurricanes that strike the United States and the Caribbean each year are stronger and more damaging than in the past.

▲ *When global warming melts the ice caps at the North and South Poles, the extra water makes the sea level rise. The people of small Pacific island states, such as Tuvalu (shown here), are severely threatened by the rising water.*

Gases in the Air

Air pollution creates environmental and health problems. Acid rain forms when water vapor in the air mixes with gases, including sulfur dioxide, to form acid, which can be as strong as lemon juice. It kills sensitive water organisms in lakes and dissolves limestone, which is a common building material. The biggest source of sulfur dioxide is industry, especially power stations. Ammonia is another harmful pollutant. A large amount of ammonia comes from the waste from livestock farms. It attacks an important layer in the atmosphere, which is rich in ozone gas. This ozone layer shields us from harmful rays from the sun that can cause skin cancer. Ammonia also creates microscopic particles in the air that can trigger asthma attacks and heart problems in some people.

◀ *Acid rain harms the plants' leaves and damages the nutrients in the soil, so less is available for plants. This causes the plants to get sick and may kill them, which has happened to these trees.*

LAND CLEARANCE

Farmers worldwide have transformed large areas of natural habitat. Low-lying wetlands have been drained, and forests destroyed, all to make way for crops or for livestock.

Habitat Loss

Draining wetlands gives farmers new areas of fertile soil on which to grow crops. But this harms the wildlife that needs damp conditions to survive, such as frogs. A third of the endangered species in the United States live in wetlands. Deforestation, or the destruction of forests, is another major problem. In Central and South America, two-thirds of deforestation is to create ranches for livestock. In Asia, many forests are being destroyed to make way for crops of palm oil and soybeans. When forests are cut down and burned, the wild animals and plants that lived there may become rare or even extinct. The lives and cultures of forest people,

▲ *Alligators can become a danger to people and pets when they lose their natural habitat of swamps and wetlands, and have to find new places to live.*

CASE STUDY

Alligators on the Move

Large numbers of American alligators live in the Everglades swamps in Florida. Much of this wetland habitat has been drained over the past century, partly to create farmland.

As a result, alligators are under threat. Changing water channels has meant there are fewer good nest sites for alligators. With less water to live in, alligators are displaced and are now often found in swimming pools, ponds, on golf courses, and in other new habitats.

▲ *This picture shows land clearance in the Amazon. According to a United Nations report, 18 million acres (7.3 million ha) of forest was lost globally every year from 2000 to 2005.*

such as the Yanomami of the Amazon region, Brazil, change forever when farmers take over forest lands. Globally, agriculture is responsible for more habitat loss than any other industry.

Biofuels

There is now more demand for farmland than ever, because farmers are growing crops to provide biofuels. Biofuels are oil and alcohol made from crops, including sugar cane and corn. Using biofuels is popular because oil, from which gasoline and diesel fuels are made, is expensive and in short supply. So many farmers are growing biofuels that they are producing less food for people and livestock. This makes food more expensive, and the poorest people cannot afford to feed themselves and their families.

ECOSYSTEM IMPACTS

Agriculture not only harms organisms in the farm environment and beyond through water pollution, soil erosion, air pollution, and habitat destruction. It also has many other impacts on wildlife and ecosystems.

Pesticides and Herbicides

Some pesticides and herbicides are designed to kill very specific pests or weeds. Others kill anything in or around the field they are sprayed on. These may include any caterpillars that birds eat, which harms the birds. Also, when farmers repeatedly use the same pesticides, or the wrong amounts, some pests become resistant and are no longer affected by pesticides. For instance, in the United States, fruit flies that damage oranges became resistant to the pesticide malathion.

Genetic Modification

Scientists have changed the genes of some crops to create new varieties that produce more food, survive better in harsh conditions, or resist herbicides. This process is called genetic modification (GM). However, some people are concerned that this may cause environmental

◀ The monarch butterflies of North America are famous for their dramatic migration: south in the fall and north in the spring. However, butterfly numbers are dropping and many scientists believe this is the result of the use of pesticides and the destruction of the plants they depend on for food.

Introducing Toads

Natural ecosystems are changed when organisms that are not native to an area are introduced. Cane toads were brought to Australia in order to eat certain beetles that destroy sugar cane. But the toads actually preferred other prey. They increased in numbers and became a pest. This is because cane toads have poisonous skin that harms or kills not only native predators, but also pets that eat the toads. People can also get sick if they touch the toads.

problems. Bees may collect pollen from GM crops and pollinate other crops or organic crops, causing cross-contamination. They also worry that genetic modification may give rise to new species of superweeds that will be hard to destroy.

Spreading Problems

On intensive farms, many animals live close together. If one catches a disease or parasite, the problem can spread quickly to other animals. For instance, farmed salmon are affected by sea lice, which damage the skin of fish reared in cages. Wild fish nearby are likely to catch the lice and suffer, too. Highly processed livestock feed can also cause problems. In the UK, between the mid-1980s and the end of the 1990s, hundreds of thousands of cattle were slaughtered because of an outbreak

of a brain disease called Bovine Spongiform Encephalopathy (BSE), which can affect humans. Scientists traced BSE to foodstuffs that contained the remains of animals such as sheep, and which had been fed to cattle to make them grow fast. These feeds have now been banned.

▶ *Cane toads are the largest kind of toad there is. They came originally from South America, but are now a major pest in Australia.*

SUSTAINABLE FARMING

Many farmers work hard to produce food without harming the environment around them. In this way, they hope to safeguard their livelihood and food production in the future. This is sustainable farming.

Low-Water Farming

Sustainable farming choices often save money. For example, planting trees creates windbreaks, which reduces soil erosion and the amounts of agrochemicals needed to maintain soil fertility. Instead of irrigating fields with sprayers, some farmers use drip irrigation, which delivers water gradually to the roots of crops. Some farmers cover soil between crops with mulches (layers of straw or plastic), to prevent not only evaporation from fields but also the growth of weeds. Even crops such as rice, which are traditionally grown by flooding fields, can grow with less water by spacing out plants and carefully managing how damp the roots become.

◀ *The straw mulch between these rows of strawberries allows rainwater to pass through it, and helps keep the soil damp, so the plants get enough moisture.*

Fewer Chemicals, Less Pollution

Organic farmers do not use any agrochemicals. They try to prevent nutrients from being washed out of the soil by planting catch crops, such as clover. These take nutrients from the soil, and release them when the plants are plowed back into soil. Organic farmers target pests without pesticides. They plant different crops on different areas of their farms over the years to prevent pests from building up in particular fields. They plant flowers that attract predators who will attack the pests.

> **Treat the Earth well: it was not given to you by your parents, it was loaned to you by your children.**
>
> Old proverb

NATURAL ADVANTAGES

In 2007, scientists Ivette Perfecto and her colleagues at Michigan University discovered that organic farming produces, at the most, a 10 percent lower yield per square mile than farming with agrochemicals. Often, the yield is higher. They calculated that a global switch to organic farming could feed the world without harming the environment.

▼ *The praying mantis is a large insect that lives in warmer parts of the world. It plays an important part in pest control by feeding on other insects.*

GLOSSARY

agrochemicals chemicals that farmers spread on their land, including fertilizers, pesticides (chemicals that kill pests such as insects), and herbicides (weed killers).

alfalfa a clover-like plant, often used as cattle feed.

algae plantlike organisms, some of which are made up of just one cell, that generally live in moist or wet conditions.

ammonia a strong-smelling gas made up of nitrogen and hydrogen.

aquifer a layer of rocks under the ground through which water flows.

bacteria (singular: **bacterium**) very tiny organisms, made up of single cells. Some cause disease, but others do useful jobs such as turning milk into yogurt.

biofuel a kind of fuel made from plants or animal waste.

calcium a substance that forms part of bones, shells, chalk, milk, and much more.

carbon dioxide a gas made up of carbon and oxygen.

carbon footprint the amount of greenhouse gases, such as carbon dioxide, released as the result of a human activity, such as producing meat.

catch crop crops grown to "catch" nutrients in the ground, so that they are not washed away by the rain.

cholera a disease caused by bacteria in polluted water, especially if there is human waste in it. It causes very serious diarrhea, and can kill.

climate the average weather a place has over several years.

dairy products foods made from milk, such as yogurt, butter, and cheese.

deforestation destroying the trees in a landscape.

desertification the process of turning land into a desert.

ecosystem the relationship between a group of living organisms and the environment they live in. It includes food supply, weather, and the organism's natural enemies.

elements the basic substances that everything in the world is made up of.

emissions something that is given off during a process.

erode/erosion to wear away/the process of wearing away.

eutrophication when excess nutrients in water cause algal bloom, oxygen loss in water, and death of water animals.

evaporate when a liquid changes to a gas.

gene the very tiny part of the cell of a living thing that tells it how it will develop.

greenhouse gas as the sun's rays heat the Earth's surface, this heat is reflected back into the atmosphere. Greenhouse gases trap it, as a greenhouse traps heat.

groundwater water that has collected deep under the ground and which may force itself to the surface as a spring, or collect in a well.

habitat the place where animals and plants naturally live.

herbicides chemicals that kill plants.

humus the dark, rich part of the soil that makes it fertile. It is made up of decayed plants.

hurricane a very violent storm, also called a tropical cyclone, when winds move at great speed around a calm center.

hydroelectric power electricity made using the power of moving water.

input anything that is put into producing things. On a farm, inputs include the labor (work) needed to grow crops and fertilizer to improve the soil.

intensive farm a farm that uses a lot of inputs to get a large output, more than the land would produce naturally.

interaction actions that influence each other.

interdependent depending on each other.

irrigation bringing water to crops from rivers or wells or another source, so that plants live and grow when there is not enough rain.

livestock farm animals, such as pigs, cattle, or sheep.

methane a gas that forms when plants decay or are digested by animals.

minerals substances found naturally in the soil.

nitrogen a gas that makes up about four-fifths of the air.

nitrous oxide a gas made up of nitrogen and oxygen.

nutrient a substance that helps a living thing to grow and live healthily.

organic farming a kind of farming that does not use agrochemicals.

organism a living thing.

ozone layer a layer of the gas ozone, which is a form of oxygen, high in the atmosphere.

phosphorus an element that is vital for plant health.

photosynthesis the process that green plants use to make the food they need to grow, using water, carbon dioxide, and the sun's energy.

pollinate to carry pollen from one plant to another, so that the plant can form seeds.

sea lice tiny shellfish that live on the skins of fish and damage them.

subsistence farmer a farmer who grows food to mainly feed his or her own family.

toxic algal bloom a growth of poisonous algae in water.

turbine an engine in which there is a wheel with vanes or paddles that will turn when forced to do so by water or wind.

wetland a swampy, boggy area of land.

TOPIC WEB, FIND OUT MORE, AND WEB SITES

FARMING AND THE ENVIRONMENT

English and Literacy
- Review newspaper articles about biofuels. What are the arguments about using them? Present these as two lists: "for" and "against."
- Research traditional sayings, especially Native American ones, about caring for the environment. Collect these and make a booklet of proverbs, with details of where the proverbs come from and what they mean.

Art and Culture
- Design a poster about the importance of the sustainable use of water, particularly in agriculture.
- Research environmental sculpture, for example, the work of Andy Goldsworthy. Try making your own environmental sculptures.

History and Economics
- Investigate the work of campaigners in the nineteenth century who tried to put a stop to food producers using additives such as chalk in bread flour or sheep dung in coffee.
- Research the organic food revolution in Cuba that started in the 1990s, and why it happened. Make a timeline of the events inside and outside Cuba that led up to the need for the food revolution.
- Look at the history of organic farming. Debate whether it is a new term for an old way of growing food.

Science and Environment
- Find out about the nitrogen cycle, which enables plants to gain access to nutrients from the air. Draw a diagram to illustrate this cycle.
- Create a flow chart to show how scientists create GM seeds. Show whom the scientists depend on to make their work possible, and who depends on the scientists to do it successfully.
- Research into the different ways in which farmers in poor countries are trying to reduce soil erosion and its effects. Make diagrams to show how the different methods they use work.

Geography
- Find out which industries, apart from farming, use up large amounts of the world's water resources. List them and explain what the industries do.
- People often destroy mangrove forest to create shrimp farms. What is the link between mangroves and coastal flooding? Show your findings as a diagram.
- Research the ways governments worldwide are reducing greenhouse gases, and trying in other ways to slow climate change. List things you can do to cut down on greenhouse gases.

FIND OUT MORE

Books

Action For The Environment: Food For All
by Rufus Bellamy (Smart Apple Media, 2009)

Can The Earth Survive?: Threats To Our Water Supply
by Louise Spilsbury (Rosen Central, 2009)

Reducing Air Pollution
by Jen Green (Gareth Stevens Publishing, 2005)

Sustainable World: Food and Farming
by Rob Bowden (Kidshaven Press, 2003)

Web Sites

Due to the changing nature of Internet links, PowerKids Press has developed an online list of Web sites related to the subject of this book. This site is updated regularly. Please use this link to access this list:
http://www.powerkidslinks.com/faf/enviro

INDEX

A
acid rain 23
agrochemicals 12, 13, 14, 15, 28, 29, 30
air 4, 14, 30, 31
    pollution of 22–23, 26, 31
algae, algal bloom 14, 15, 30
alligators 24
ammonia 20, 23, 30
aquifers 8, 10, 30

B
bacteria 14, 15, 16, 20, 30
bees 6, 7, 27
Bovine Spongiform Encephalopathy (BSE) 27

C
cane toads 27
carbon
    dioxide 4, 20, 21, 22, 30
    footprint 20, 30
cattle, cows 6, 9, 27, 30

D
dairy products 8, 30
deforestation 19, 24, 30
deserts, desertification 18, 30
dust 18
Dust Bowl 19

E
ecosystems 4–5, 6, 14, 19, 26–27, 30
erosion 16–17, 18–19, 26, 28, 30, 31

eutrophication 14, 30
evaporation 9, 28, 30

F
farm machinery 20, 21
fertilizers 4, 12, 13, 15, 30
fish 6, 11, 14, 27, 30
    farming 6, 27
    fishermen 11
    fishing, 10
forests, forestry 5, 17, 21, 24, 25, 31

G
genetic modification 26,27
global warming 22, 23
greenhouse gases 20, 21, 22, 23, 30, 31

H
herbicides 12, 26, 30

I
industry 10, 19, 20, 21, 23, 25, 31
intensive farms 13, 27, 30
interdependence 6–7, 30
irrigation 4, 8, 9, 11, 14, 28, 30

L
lakes 8, 10, 14, 23
    Lake Chad 11

M
manure 12, 13, 20

N
nitrates 12, 14, 15
nutrients 4, 5, 6, 11, 12, 16,

17, 23, 29, 30, 31

O
oceans 6, 23
organic farming 27, 29, 30, 31
overgrazing 18, 19
oxygen 14, 30
ozone layer 23, 30

P
pesticides 4, 12, 26, 29, 30
phosphates 12, 14
photosynthesis 4, 20, 30
pollination 6, 7, 27, 30
pollution 6, 10, 12–13, 14–15, 22–23, 26, 29, 30, 31
praying mantis 29

R
rain, rainfall 4, 5, 6, 8, 10, 11, 13, 17, 19, 23, 28, 30
rivers 6, 8, 10, 13, 14, 19, 30
runoff 13

S
salination 11
slurry 13, 15
sustainable farming 28–29, 31

T
toxic algal bloom 14, 30

W
water 4, 5, 8, 9, 10, 11, 13, 14, 16, 22, 23, 24, 28, 30, 31
    demand for 8–9, 28
    overuse of 10–11
    pollution of 6, 12–13, 14–15, 19, 23, 26
wind 9, 16, 17, 28, 30